The World of Whales

Get to Know the Giants of the Ocean

LITTLE GESTALTEN

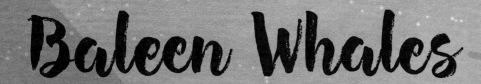

Baleen Whales

Toothed Whales

Dall's Porpoise

Vaquita

Harbour Porpoise

Cuvier's Beaked Whale pp. 44–45
Beluga Whale pp. 24–25
Dolphin pp. 28–29
Sperm Whale pp. 40–41

When the sounds hit an object,
such as a school of fish,
they bounce back to the whales.
From these echoes the whales
can work out the shape,
size, and distance of the object.
They can even tell if it is a
living creature, such as a fish, or
a hard surface such as a rock.

The clicks travel out through
the flexible front part of
the whales' heads, or the melons.
By changing the shape
of their melons, belugas can aim
the clicks at an object
in the water, which is a bit like
pointing a sonic laser beam
at something.

Dolphins

— A playful pod —

A group of dolphins rise and dive as they speed along. These playful animals, with their long snouts, curved fins, and "smiling" mouths, are easy to spot. They can be found in all the world's oceans, and even in some rivers.

Friends and family

Dolphins often travel in large groups, called pods, sometimes joining other kinds of dolphins and whales, too. A pod of dolphins fills the water with the sounds of whistles, chirps, and squeals. Dolphins also use their bodies to communicate: they slap their tails on the water and stroke one another with their fins.

Did you know?

Dolphins make up the largest branch of the family of toothed whales.

Beyond the sea

Sink beneath the surface of this wide river and you might spot an unusual sight: a river dolphin moving slowly through the muddy water. Unlike its ocean cousins, it usually swims alone, searching for fish to eat. River dolphins are found in just a few rivers in the world.

Yangtze RIVER

Ganges RIVER

Amazon RIVER

Ocean acrobats

Dolphins leap high out of the water, turning flips and somersaults in the air. Some can stand on their tails and "walk" backwards on the water. They even team up with dolphin buddies to perform together in perfect harmony. The spinner dolphin is the most acrobatic of all. Count the turns as it leaps into the air—1, 2, 3, 4, 5, 6, 7!

1 .. 2 .. 3 .. 4 5 6 .. 7!

Lively learners

Although they have no hands, dolphins have found ways to make tools. A group of spotted dolphins in Australia has learned to rip sponges from the seafloor to wear on their beaks. The soft sponges protect the dolphins as they poke for fish among the spiky rocks and corals. Some bottlenose dolphins also make their own toys by blowing bubble rings in the water, swimming through them, and even passing them back and forth to one another.

Bowhead Whale

— A marine musician —

Welcome to the Arctic, one of the coldest places on Earth. Deep below the frozen sea, bowhead whales cruise along like big, gray submarines, looking to fuel up on food.

Bowhead whales have no dorsal fin or hump. Having a flat back means they can glide along under the ice.

To stay warm, bowheads have a thick layer of oily fat, called blubber. This can grow to be more than 2ft (0.6m) thick around their middles.

Bowheads get their name from their huge upper jaws, which are shaped like an archer's bow. They have the largest mouth of any animal.

Cool sounds

You probably wouldn't want to put your head under water in the Arctic Ocean during the cold, dark months of winter. But if you did, you might hear some remarkable sounds. Bowhead whales sing for hours at a time, performing a wide variety of groans, whistles, and wails. They create a new set of songs each year.

Ice-breakers

Bowhead whales are usually found in and around the Arctic Ocean's ice. Like all whales, they need to come to the surface to breathe. They can use their powerful heads to smash breathing holes through ice that is as thick as a mattress. Scientists think the whales listen to the echoes from their calls to work out how thick the ice is. This way, they can avoid ice that is too solid to break.

Did you know?

These powerful whales can live to be more than 200 years old. They are one of the longest-living mammals in the world.

Length: **up to 60 feet (18 meters)**

Weight: **up to 100 tons (90 tonnes)**

Blue Whale

— The largest animal on Earth —

Imagine being out at sea when a huge, dark shape comes looming out of the gloom. It's bigger than the biggest dinosaur, longer than three buses, and as heavy as 40 adult elephants. You have just met the largest animal on Earth! But don't worry, you are far too big for this mega mammal to eat.

Did you know?

A newborn blue whale is the size of a full-grown elephant.

Super-sounds

The blue whale has a big voice to match its size. It makes all sorts of noises, from clicks and hums to rumbling grumbles. Its calls can reach 180 decibels, which is much louder than the roar of a jumbo jet taking off. In fact, the blue whale is the loudest animal in the world, but even so, you might not be able to hear it. Its long, low calls can be so deep that they are below the range of human hearing.

Web of Life

— Everything is connected —

Blue whales are the biggest animals in the world, but they feed on some of the littlest, including tiny fish and krill. A single whale can eat several tons of food every day. That's more than 40 million krill!

Even though they eat so much, a sea full of whales is a good thing for krill and fish. Many of the things whales do help to keep the oceans healthy and full of life.

Plankton

When the sun shines on the sea, tiny floating seaweeds called plankton can grow and spread. Plankton is the main food for krill and small fish.

Whales that hunt far below the waves will come to the surface to breathe. They will often poop before they dive again. Whale poop is full of nutrition from the deep sea and is an important source of food for tiny plants and creatures that live near the surface.

When whales feed, they often drive schools of fish up to the surface of the sea. This helps seabirds, who can now reach them, too. Flocks of seabirds will gather around feeding whales.

Krill and copepods

These little shrimp-like creatures are not much bigger than a paperclip, but they are a main food source for all sorts of animals, from fish and seabirds to gigantic baleen whales.

On the seafloor

When a whale dies, its body sinks to the bottom of the sea. Now it is food for small fish and shrimp. The fallen whale also becomes food for corals and sponges, which build reefs that many little fish and shellfish live in.

Seabirds bring fish back to their nests to feed their chicks. As they fly back and forth, they often poop over the land and water. Seabird poop makes good food for plants on land, and helps the plankton to grow at sea.

Food for all

Small fish feed on plankton, and larger fish feed on small fish. Whales, dolphins, porpoises, and many other animals hunt the larger fish. Many different kinds of animals may gather together in areas where there are lots of fish to eat.

Tiny bits of the dead whale are carried by currents back to the surface, where they become plant food, helping new plankton to grow.

Sea to Sky

Although whales breathe air, they cannot live on land. In the ocean they can swim gracefully, held up by the water, but up on the shore, their bulky bodies are much too heavy to move around. But this does not stop them from exploring some of the world beyond their watery home.

Sneaking a peek

A whale can poke its head out of the water to take a look around. This is called spy-hopping. Because most whales cannot bend their necks, a spy-hopping whale must hold its body straight up in the water. Orcas often spy-hop while they are hunting animals such as seals on the shoreline.

Whale of a tail

Sometimes a whale will lift its tail high out of the water and then bring it down with a mighty WHACK! This is called lobtailing and can be used to stun fish, or to communicate with other whales, since the ear-splitting smack can be heard a long way away.

Flip-flop

Some whales and dolphins will slap the water with their flippers. Humpback whales sometimes lie on their backs, lift up one or both of their long, flexible flippers, and then roll from side to side so that each flipper hits the water over and over again.

Time to fly

When a whale is moving fast, chasing prey, or escaping from danger, it needs to stay close to the surface to breathe often. At high speeds, leaping through the air can be easier than traveling through water, so it zooms along performing shallow leaps and dives. This is called porpoising.

Making waves

When a whale launches most, or all, of its body out of the water, it is breaching. It lands with a huge SPLASH, sending a shock wave through the water that can be heard by other whales many miles away. Whales may breach to clean themselves, knocking barnacles or other creatures off their skin. Breaching may also be a way of communicating with other whales.

Sperm Whale
— The brainiest animal ever —

If you spot a wrinkly-skinned whale with a huge, square head, you are looking at one of the most enormous animals on Earth—a sperm whale. This block-headed mammal is full of surprises. It has the biggest brain the world has ever seen. It doesn't attack people, but if you happen to be a squid, beware—this brainy predator is coming to get you!

Code names

Sperm whales make a sharp "clang" that can be as loud as a rocket taking off. When they call out to one another, sperm whales use patterns of clicks called codas. Each group of sperm whales has its own coda.

Length: up to 60 feet (17 meters)

Weight: up to 45 tons (41 tonnes)

Busy moms

Female sperm whales stick together in pods of up to 20 whales. They take turns babysitting one another's calves at the surface while the mothers dive for food. If predators such as orcas threaten their calves, the whales arrange themselves in a flower shape around their young.

Did you know?

The sperm whale is the biggest of the toothed whales, making it the largest animal with teeth in the world.

Nose dive

The big brain is not the only remarkable thing in a sperm whale's head. The front of the head is a huge sac filled with oily wax called spermaceti, which may help to focus the beams of sound it uses to hunt and communicate.

Sperm whales use their powerful tails for swimming and protection.

The blowhole sits on the left side of a sperm whale's head.

A sperm whale's head can make up almost one-third of its body length.

Sperm whales have small flippers that tuck in close to their bodies during deep dives.

Their lower jaws are lined with teeth that can grow up to 8 inches (20cm) long.

41

Whale Research

— Studying what you cannot see —

Imagine if scientists decided to study you by looking just at your nose. How much do you think they could learn about your life? Whales spend most of their lives under water, out of sight. We can only get glimpses of parts of their bodies. While watching whales at the surface of the water is important, researchers must also use other tools to study what is happening beneath the waves.

What a whiff

Researchers wave nets, or fly drones, through whale blow and even whale poo to gather samples to study. They may be smelly, but these samples provide valuable information about what the whales are eating and how healthy they are. Some researchers use trained dogs to help sniff out whale poo on the surface of the sea.

Listen up

Underwater microphones, called hydrophones, allow researchers to listen in to whale calls. This is useful for learning about how whales "talk" to each other. Because hydrophones can also record where and when different whales are calling, they help to show how whales move around.

Whales in captivity

Some researchers study whales, dolphins, and porpoises in aquariums. The close-up view has helped scientists learn more about how these animals live and play together, as well as how they communicate and use echolocation. But other researchers argue that it's wrong to separate whales from their family groups and to keep such intelligent and active wild animals in tiny pools.

Cuvier's Beaked Whale

— The champion of the deep dive —

Ready to go diving with a record-breaking mammal? Take a deep breath and plunge into the mysterious depths of the ocean with a Cuvier's beaked whale. It can stay under water for more than two hours while it hunts for squid and fish, but you are probably gasping for air already!

Breathtaking

If you were going to dive under water, you would start by taking a big, deep breath in. Cuvier's beaked whales do the opposite: before a long dive, these whales blow out almost all of the air in their lungs. Air makes things float, so without it, the whales can sink faster and use less energy to dive. Instead of taking oxygen from the air in their lungs, they use oxygen stored in their muscles.

Length: **up to 23 feet (7 meters)**

Weight: **up to 2.7 tons (2.5 tonnes)**

Deep down

Cuvier's beaked whales often hunt up to 1 mile (1.5 km) under the sea. One was tracked as it dove to nearly 2 miles (3 km)—the deepest dive by a mammal ever recorded.

Far out

Cuvier's beaked whales are the most common of the beaked whales, but they are still hard to spot. That is because they prefer to stay where the ocean is deepest, far from shore.

The heads and backs of adult males are usually covered in scars, probably caused by the tusks of other males. Researchers use the patterns of scars to identify the whales.

Like other toothed whales, Cuvier's beaked whales have a single blowhole.

They have short flippers that can tuck into little hollows called "flipper pockets." They tuck their flippers in tightly when they dive.

Although they are classed as toothed whales, they hardly have any teeth at all. Adult males have just two short tusks that poke out from their lower jaws. Females and young whales have none.

Did you know?

As they don't have any teeth, Cuvier's beaked whales cannot bite their prey. Instead, they catch squid or fish by slurping them out of the water and then swallowing them whole.

45

Looking After Baby

A mother whale strokes her newborn baby with her flipper. She will do everything she can to protect and care for her baby. There is a lot to learn about life in the ocean and the baby will meet many dangers along the way, but its mother will be close by its side until it grows to be big and strong, just like her.

A little help

When you were small, a grown-up could carry you when you were tired. Whale mothers can't pick up their babies, but they do have a way of carrying them around. When the mother whale swims, her large body makes a current in the water. The baby whale stays close enough to its mother to be lifted and carried along in her current. The baby can even sleep or nurse while its mother swims.

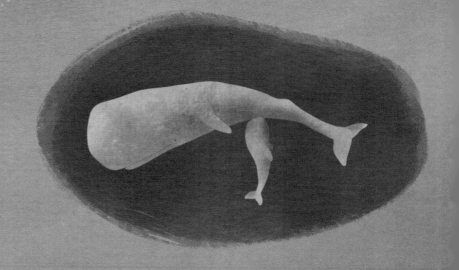

Born to swim

Baby whales are born under water, so the very first thing they must do is swim to the surface to take a breath of air. They are usually born tail first, which helps them to be ready to swim right away.

Baby food

Whale milk is very fatty, which helps the baby grow a layer of blubber. A very young baby whale can only feed from the mother for a short time before having to go up to the surface for a breath.

Krill Tiny sea animals that look like small shrimp. Krill are a main food source for baleen whales as well as many seabirds and fish. They are an essential part of the ocean food web. Without them, most of the larger sea animals would not exist.

Mammals The group of animals that feed milk to their babies, with most giving birth to their babies instead of laying eggs. Mammals range in size from tiny shrews and humans to blue whales.

Migration The movement of animals over long distances. Many animals migrate with the seasons, spending winter in one place and summer in another. Migration helps animals to reach good feeding grounds and safe places to have their babies.

Oxygen The colorless gas that all animals and plants need in order to live. Oxygen is produced by plants as they grow. Half of the oxygen in every breath you take is made by plankton in the ocean.

Plankton Tiny living organisms including animals, plants, and seaweeds that live in the sea. Plankton that are plants or seaweeds are called phytoplankton, while plankton that are animals are called zooplankton.

Pod The name for a group of whales. Some whales are found in small pods made up of a few family members, while others travel in large pods that can number in the hundreds.

Pollution The act of putting damaging material into the world around us. Pollution makes water, land, and air unhealthy. Plastic is one example of pollution in our oceans. We can help to keep the oceans healthy by using less plastic and by picking up rubbish wherever we go.

Predator An animal that kills and eats other animals in order to live. Examples include lions, hawks, spiders, and orcas.

School A large group of fish moving through the water together. A school of fish that has stopped moving—to feed, for example—is called a shoal.

Snout The projecting nose and mouth of an animal, especially a mammal.

Spermaceti A white waxy substance that is found in the head of a sperm whale and may help the whale to echolocate and navigate. People once used spermaceti in makeup, perfumes, candles, and ointments.

Ton A unit of mass used in the United States. A ton is 2,000 pounds.

🚗 = 1.4 ton

🚌 = 14 tons

Tonne (metric ton) A unit of mass used outside the United States. A tonne is 1,000 kilogram, or 2,204.6 pounds.

Tusk A long tooth that has developed to be a weapon or a sense organ, or just for display.

Whales A general term for members of the cetacean family, often used to refer to whales, dolphins, and porpoises together. Whales are large, air-breathing mammals that spend their entire lives in the water. They are found in all of the oceans and in some rivers.

Left: One of the modern housing developments close to Paris.

Below: Strasbourg, in Alsace, is an old cathedral city and river port. It has a strong Germanic influence as it is near the border with Germany.

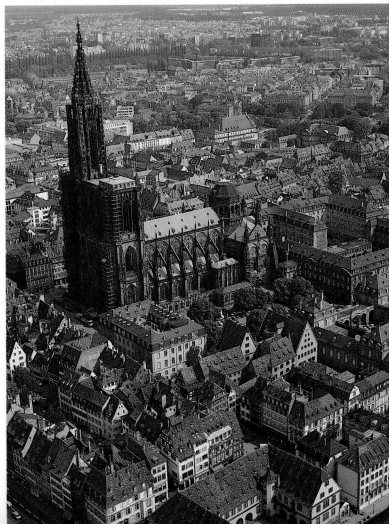

Paris, with its "satellite" towns, is the largest urban area in Europe outside the Soviet Union. Many of its people live in modern housing developments in such new towns as Marne-la-Vallée.

In comparison with Paris, other French cities are only medium sized. There are only two cities, Marseille and Lyon, which, with their surrounding districts, have more than a million inhabitants, and three (Lille, Bordeaux and Toulouse) with over 500,000.

The provincial cities and towns cannot match the cultural attractions of Paris. But many contain outstanding historic buildings, notably medieval cathedrals. In these ancient towns old houses, lacking modern facilities, are often found alongside new developments.

Apart from television aerials and modern traffic, many small villages in rural areas throughout France still look the way they did centuries ago. Houses with shuttered windows face directly on to a main street, which often opens into a square enclosed by a church, small shops and outdoor cafés.

Paris

Paris, the capital of France, is the nation's government, business and cultural heart. It is also one of the world's most beautiful cities, with elegant boulevards, spacious squares and impressive buildings and monuments. There are also many fine hotels, shops, restaurants and places of entertainment. Paris also has busy traffic, for it is a bustling, working city that lies in a major industrial region.

In area Paris is not a large city and only 2 million people live in the city itself. Nearly 9 million people, however, live in the Greater Paris area.

The River Seine winds through Paris for about 13 km (8 miles), enclosed by high stone embankments and crossed by many bridges. The city spreads out on each side around the historic Ile de la Cité (City Isle). Here Paris was founded by Celtic peoples more than 2,000 years ago. As it grew, the city was encircled several times by walls. But these are long gone, and on their site there are now broad, tree-lined boulevards built to a grand plan between 1853 and 1870.

Above: The Eiffel Tower, a famous Paris landmark, dominates the city's skyline. It rises to a height of 320 m (1,056 ft).

Below: Some of the most popular sights to visit in Paris. Paris hosts many of the 30 million visitors every year to France.

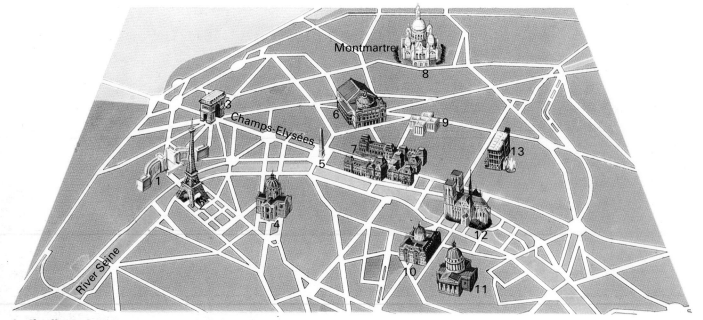

1 Chaillot Palace	5 Place de la Concord	9 The Bourse (Stock Exchange)	12 Notre Dame
2 Eiffel Tower	6 Opera	10 Luxembourg Palace	13 Pompidou Center
3 Arc de Triomphe	7 The Louvre	11 Panthéon	
4 Invalides	8 Sacré-Cœur		

Several low hills rise above some parts of Paris. The highest, in Montmartre, reaches 130 m (426 ft). On it stands one of the city's best-known landmarks, the church of Sacré Cœur (Sacred Heart).

Many other places of interest are scattered around the city, most of them easily reached by the underground subway system, called the Métro. Among the most popular are the Eiffel Tower, the Louvre, the Tuileries Gardens, the Arc de Triomphe and the Pompidou Center cultural complex. There are also such interesting sights as the richly ornamented Opera House and the Elysée Palace, the official residence of the French president.

Many people particularly enjoy the lively atmosphere of the Latin Quarter, the students' district on the left bank of the Seine. Others prefer the peaceful surroundings of the Luxembourg Gardens or the pleasant woods of the Bois de Boulogne.

Above: The Champs-Elysées is the most famous of the boulevards that radiate from the Arc de Triomphe in central Paris.

Below: The pleasant Tuileries Gardens occupy the site of a former royal palace near the Louvre Museum.

Fact file: land and population

Key facts

Location: France is on the western edge of the continent of Europe between latitudes 42° and 51° North.

Main parts: France contains 22 Metropolitan regions—21 on mainland France and the island of Corsica. France also has five Overseas Departments: Guadeloupe in the West Indies; French Guiana in South America; Martinique in the West Indies; Réunion in the Indian Ocean; and St Pierre and Miquelon, a group of islands off the coast of Newfoundland, Canada.

Area: 547,026 sq km (211,208 sq miles), not including Overseas Departments.

Population: 55,623,000 (1987 estimate).

Capital: Paris.

Major cities:
Paris (city, 2,189,000; city and suburbs, 8,707,000).
Other leading cities (with their city and suburb populations):
Lyon (1,221,000)
Marseille (1,111,000)
Lille (936,000)
Bordeaux (640,000)
Toulouse (541,000)
Nantes (465,000)
Nice (449,000)

Main languages: French (official). Other languages include Alsatian, a form of German (Alsace region); Basque (in the southwest); Breton (in Brittany); Catalan (western end of Mediterranean coast); and Provençal (southeast).

Highest point: Mont Blanc in the French Alps, 4,807 m (15,771 ft).

Longest rivers:
Loire, 1,010 km (628 miles)
Rhône, 810 km (503 miles)
Seine, 770 km (478 miles)
Garonne, 650 km (404 miles)

Largest lake:
Lac du Bourget, east of Lyon, 43 sq km (16.6 sq miles).

France has four main climatic types: *temperate marine* near the northern and western coasts, *Continental* in central areas, *Mountains*, and *Mediterranean* near the southern coasts.

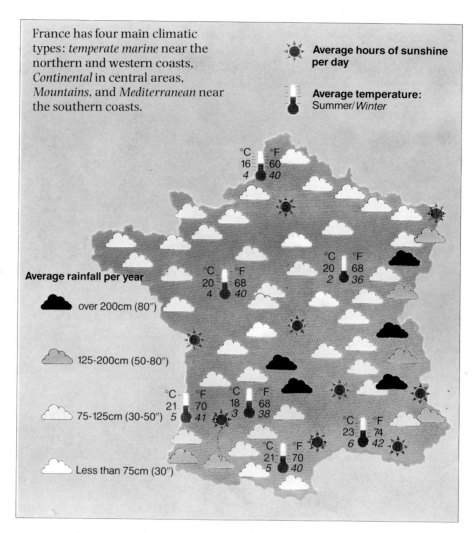

Average hours of sunshine per day

Average temperature: Summer/*Winter*

Average rainfall per year

over 200cm (80″)

125-200cm (50-80″)

75-125cm (30-50″)

Less than 75cm (30″)

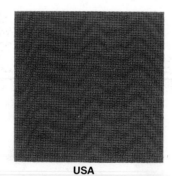

USA   **AUSTRALIA**   **FRANCE**   **GREAT BRITAIN**

△ **A land area comparison**
France's 547,026 sq km (211,208 sq miles) of land is small as against that of countries such as the U.S.A. with 9,370,000 sq km (3,600,000 sq miles) and Australia with 7,650,000 sq km (2,470,000 sq miles). In European terms France is a large country. Great Britain, for example, has only 229,979 sq km (88,759 sq miles) of land. France has roughly the same land area as Great Britain, the former West Germany, Belgium and the Netherlands all put together. Its coastline is 3,427 km (2,129 miles) including 644 km (400 miles) of Corsica.

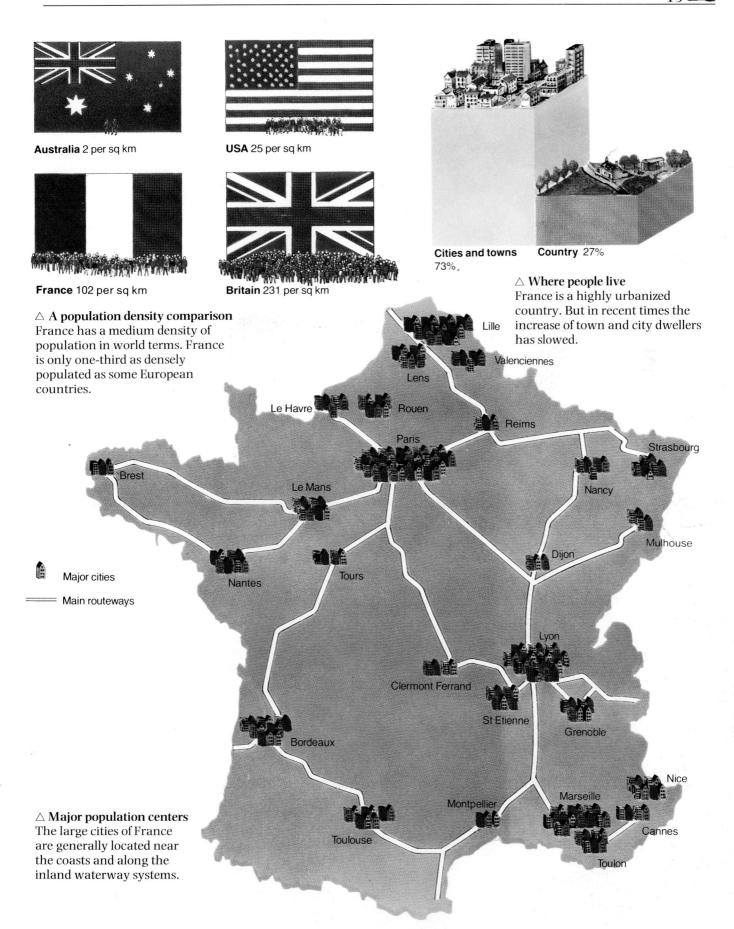

Australia 2 per sq km

USA 25 per sq km

France 102 per sq km

Britain 231 per sq km

Cities and towns 73%

Country 27%

△ **Where people live**
France is a highly urbanized country. But in recent times the increase of town and city dwellers has slowed.

△ **A population density comparison**
France has a medium density of population in world terms. France is only one-third as densely populated as some European countries.

Lille

Valenciennes

Lens

Le Havre

Rouen

Reims

Strasbourg

Paris

Brest

Nancy

Le Mans

Mulhouse

Dijon

Nantes

Tours

Major cities

Main routeways

Lyon

Clermont Ferrand

St Etienne

Grenoble

Bordeaux

Nice

Montpellier

Marseille

△ **Major population centers**
The large cities of France are generally located near the coasts and along the inland waterway systems.

Toulouse

Cannes

Toulon

Home life

Family life is highly valued in France. Traditionally, the home contained several generations—grandparents, parents and children. But in recent years families have become smaller. Three-fifths of them now have only two or three children. Also, many children now leave home when they marry, although most live less than 20 km (12 miles) from their parents' homes.

Family ties always remain strong. Students usually go to local universities. Holidays, anniversaries and birthdays are times for family reunions.

Most French people in urban areas live in flats, which are usually rented. Many people have homes only a short distance from their place of work. Most people like modern homes which are easy to heat and clean. But they also like antique furniture, even though it may not be so comfortable.

Above: Bernadette and Guy Scoarnec live in Ivry near Paris. Guy is an architect and Bernadette is taking a university course. They are seen in front of their flat.

Right: The Scoarnec family sitting room is plain yet fashionable.

Left: The children's bedroom. As space is limited it also serves as their playroom.

Below: Bernadette Scoarnec notes down shopping requirements for the next day.

The French are a hard-working people and many work long hours of overtime in order to earn more money. The average working week in 1985 was 39 hours. About two out of every three women go to work, mainly in service industries. While at work, they may leave their younger children in nurseries, which are partly paid for by the government.

There is not much time for leisure at the end of a working day. After the evening meal most people stay at home and watch television, listen to the radio or read the newspapers or a book. Some enjoy playing cards at home, while others like to go to the local café to meet friends and talk. Children usually have a lot of homework to do each evening during the week and many are not allowed to watch television before finishing it.

Since the 1960s many working people have had more time for leisure at weekends, because the factories now close on Saturday mornings. Nearly a third of all French people now spend some time gardening. Home improvements and cooking have also become popular pastimes for many people.

Shops and shopping

The French are very demanding shoppers who like to choose their goods with care. They would never hesitate to return a rotten apple or any other imperfect item to the shopkeeper. They know the best shops follow the motto "The customer is king."

Nearly all French towns have a market. French people love elbowing their way around the stalls looking for the best buys. The stalls sell almost every kind of food, cheap clothes and all sorts of household articles. Larger towns often have specialized markets that sell only flowers, for example. Paris has a "flea market" where a great variety of old household articles can be bought. Markets are held every morning or perhaps twice a week, depending on the size of town.

At village markets local farmers often sell their own produce directly to customers from their trucks. For example, they sell fresh cheese, dairy products, honey and eggs. Village markets are held only once or twice a week. Market day is an exciting event, and the streets and cafés become crowded.

Above and **below left:** Markets are a traditional and still important part of French shopping.

Below: Some of the many types of French bread. Most people buy their bread fresh each day from the local baker.

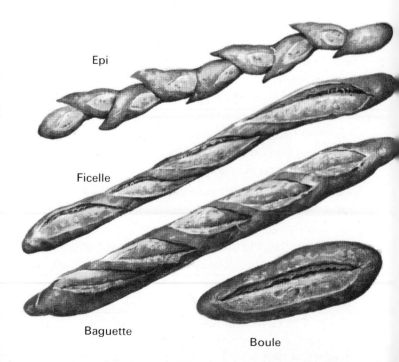

Epi

Ficelle

Baguette

Boule

Many people, particularly the elderly, prefer small local shops. Most of these have been run for many years by the same families, who get to know their customers personally. Shoppers enjoy a friendly chat while making their purchases.

France has a large number of small shops that specialize in one kind of product. These include the *boulangerie* (bread), *boucherie* (meat), *charcuterie* (cooked meats and sausages) and *épicerie* (groceries). Most small shops are closed between noon and 2 p.m., but stay open until 7 or 8 in the evening.

Many people prefer to shop in the big supermarkets and even bigger hypermarkets often found on the outskirts of towns. Here they can find everything, from a loaf of bread to household furniture. The goods are cheap and generally of high quality. All these markets have big parking lots and many are open from about 10 in the morning until 10 at night.

Above: A *charcuterie* offers a tempting range of cold meats, ready-prepared dishes and many types of sausages.

Below: The French welcome the convenience of packaged food and few now insist that all food should be freshly prepared.

Cooking and eating

The French love good food and especially enjoy talking about it. For them, cooking is an art that greatly adds to their enjoyment of life. French *cuisine*, or cooking, is famous throughout the world. There are two main types—*haute cuisine*, which uses only the finest ingredients prepared by master chefs, and *provincal*, the traditional cooking of the regions.

Although meals in French restaurants may need a lot of elaborate preparation, everyday cooking at home is quick, simple and tasty. A meal may consist of several courses, eaten with slices of fresh, crusty bread and accompanied by wine.

For the main course, cuts of meat, such as steaks or chops, may be fried with garlic and sprinkled with parsley or mixed herbs. Vegetables are served as a separate course. They are first lightly cooked and then perhaps fried with bacon and onions or sprinkled with cheese and baked in the oven. After the main course may come a fresh green salad or a selection of cheeses, followed by fruit or a dessert.

Above: The Scoarnec's kitchen is compact with the most modern equipment.

Below: The Scoarnec family sits down to a simple meal of fresh salad and a selection of cheeses.

Meal time is a special occasion for French people. They like to gather around the table as a family to chat as well as to eat. Breakfast generally consists only of *café noir* (black coffee) for the adults and *café au lait* (coffee with milk) for the children, with bread and jam. Pastry *croissants* are often eaten as a special treat for Sunday breakfast. For most families, lunch is the main meal of the day. Dinner, eaten at about 7 p.m., is a lighter meal.

Working people who cannot go home for lunch often prefer to eat a French-style sandwich in a café rather than a snack in a fast-food restaurant. French people sometimes like to dine in a restaurant with their family or friends on weekday evenings or Sunday lunchtimes, when they can take their time.

Restaurants in France generally welcome children of all ages, even if the chef has to make special courses for them. Then the dining room becomes more noisy and livelier than usual.

Above: Many restaurants are small family-run businesses which offer good food in simple surroundings.

Below: French chefs take great pride in their work and create their own specialities. A good chef is held in high regard.

Pastimes and sports

Soccer is by far the most popular sporting activity in France today, but traditional sports, such as shooting and fishing, are also enjoyed by millions of people. Tennis and riding, once the sports only of rich people, are growing rapidly in popularity, as are sailing and windsurfing.

In addition to people who like to take part in sports, there are also those who prefer to watch. Crowds of spectators flock to professional league soccer matches and games played by the French national team. Others attend rugby football matches, including the annual international game for the "Triple Crown" between France, England, Scotland, Wales and Ireland.

Another popular spectator sport is horse racing at such race tracks as Longchamps. Motor racing also draws large crowds for such famous events as the Le Mans 24-hour race, the Monte Carlo Rally and Grand Prix races. But perhaps the best-known event of all is the Tour de France cycle race, held since 1903, which tests the endurance of even the fittest riders.

Above: Boules is a traditional French game played with metal balls on any suitable patch of gravel or reasonably flat surface.

Below: Bicycle races are a major attraction. The Tour de France covers 4,000 km (2,500 miles) through the major regions of France over a three week period.

Left: Les Ménuires is one of the many busy ski resorts in the French Alps.

Below: Windsurfing has become very popular at many southern French resorts. This is Cassis on the Mediterranean coast.

Many French people particularly like sporting vacations and enjoy skiing and other winter sports in the mountains. In the summer months the mountains are also popular with climbers and hikers, and the country's many fine camping sites are generally crowded.

French people can pursue such outdoor activities more easily today, partly because they now have the right to five weeks' annual vacations with pay. As a result, people are taking several breaks at different times of the year to follow many different interests instead of just the traditional month's vacation at the beach.

The mass exodus of people in August from the towns to seaside resorts, however, still continues. The roads to the south are clogged with traffic and the beaches are crowded. The government is promoting many schemes to avoid the loss of production in August and the pressure on the resorts.

Cultural vacations exploring the history, arts and crafts of France have recently grown in popularity. Regional tourist boards are also active in the promotion of special events in their areas.

News and broadcasting

France has a very sophisticated public broadcasting system and a dynamic publishing industry. Nearly half of all French people read a newspaper every day. 86 daily newspapers are published throughout France, 14 of them in Paris. The top sellers are *France-Soir, Le Monde* and *Le Figaro* among the Paris dailies, and *Ouest-France, Le Progrès* (Lyon) and *Sud-Ouest* among the regional newspapers. Nearly 7 million of the 9.2 million newspapers sold each day are published in the regions of France.

Weekly news magazines, such as the top-selling *Paris-Match, L'Express* and *Le Nouvel Observateur* are becoming increasingly popular. Also gaining in readership are technical and economic journals and specialist magazines on leisure interests, sports and home improvement. But the weekly radio and television magazines sell most copies. French people buy about 3 million copies of *Télé 7 Jours* every week.

Above: National daily newspapers play an influential role in communication and opinion-making.

Left: News and current affairs are a favourite topic of conversation and discussion in the French café. Many people read the morning paper there, while having breakfast.

Left: Weekly magazines provide a pictorial insight into French and world events. Fashion is a very popular interest.

Above: A wide range of magazines and comics for the young are available. Astérix, a comic-strip character, is particularly popular.

The French also enjoy reading books, and book publishing is a major industry. Every year about 26,000 books are published, and over 360 million copies are printed. About a third of these are paperbacks, including detective stories and spy thrillers. Each title sells for the same price, whether it is bought in a bookshop or large store, or through a book club or mail order firm.

French people spend an average of 32 hours a week watching television and listening to the radio. The public television service provides three channels: TF1, Antenne 2 and FR3. There is also a private fourth channel, Canal Plus, which mostly shows films.

Radio programs are broadcast by the national corporation (Radio-France) and by local stations throughout France. Listeners can also tune in to French-language programs broadcast by Radio Luxembourg, Radio Monte Carlo, Europe 1 (from the Saar), Sud Radio (from Andorra) and other foreign stations.

Above: Pierre Bellemare is a popular television game show personality.

Left: *Télé 7 Jours* lists what is going to be shown on television during the coming week. A typical day's viewing presents a mixture of French and imported programs.

Fact file: home life and leisure

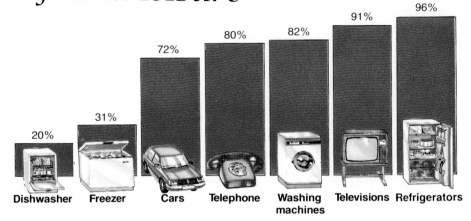

Dishwasher	Freezer	Cars	Telephone	Washing machines	Televisions	Refrigerators
20%	31%	72%	80%	82%	91%	96%

Key facts

Population composition: People under 20 years of age make up 29 per cent of the population; people between 20 and 64 make up 57 per cent; and people over 65 years make up to 14 per cent.

Average life expectancy: 77 years (1986), as compared with 72 years in 1970. Women make up 51.2 per cent of the population of France, as compared with 48.8 per cent men. This is because the average life expectancy for women is 80 years, 6 years more than for men.

Rate of population increase: 0.5 per cent per year in 1980–87, as compared with 1.1 per cent a year in 1960–70.

Family life: The average age when men marry is 25 years, as opposed to 23 years for women. The average number of children per family is 0.9. In the late 1980s, 60 per cent of French people take their vacations away from home, for an average of 30 days a year.

Homes: 50.7 per cent of French people own their main homes and about 54 per cent of these homeowners live in houses, as opposed to apartments.

Work: In 1982, the statutory working week was reduced from 40 hours to 39 hours. The workforce in 1985 was 23,886,000. In 1987, there were 2,592,700 registered job seekers. This was about one tenth of the workforce.

Prices: Prices rose by 8.0 per cent per year in 1965–1980 and by 8.8 per cent a year between 1980 and 1986.

Religions: The government does not officially recognize any church, but the largest is the Roman Catholic Church, which had an estimated 42.35 million members in 1986, though less than one-fifth were regular church attenders. In 1986, Protestants numbered about 800,000, and there were also about 2.5 million Muslims.

Leisure and arts	6·5%
Clothing and footwear	6·6%
Household goods and services	9·3%
Health	12·8%
Other goods and services	13%
Transport and Communications	13·6%
Housing	17%
Food and drink	21·2%

△ **How many households owned goods in the 1980s**
Many French homes have acquired new types of household goods in recent years. The biggest increase has been in television sets, ownership of which rose from 10 per cent to 90 per cent in 20 years. The ownership of dishwaters increased from 2.4 per cent in 1970 to 20 per cent in 1983.

◁ **How the average household budget was spent in the 1980s**
The proportion spent on food dropped from 36 per cent in 1958 to about one-fifth in the 1980s. Increases have been seen in spending on housing, health, transportation and leisure items.

▽ **French currency and stamps**
The French currency, the franc, is divided into 100 centimes. In 1985 there were about 8 francs to the US dollar.

▽ How an average family spends a working day

Midnight
12
11 1
10 2
9 3
8 4
7 5
6 6
5 7
4 8
3 9
2 10
1 11
12
Midday

Television
Reading
Dinner
Homework
Leisure
Finish work
Finish school
Sleep
Breakfast
Start school
Start work

▽ How often the most popular leisure pursuits were done in the 1980s

At least three times a week

Reading newspapers	Reading books	Watch television	Sit outside the house
76%		33%	13%

At least once a week

Knit or sew	Listen to music	Talk to friends	Gardening
84%	59%	49%	42%

At least once a month

Visit or entertain friends	Walk or cycle	Cinema	Sport
55%	36%	30%	16%

44%
Seaside

25%
Country

16%
Mountains

8%
Tours

7%
Towns

◁ **How vacations are spent**
Most families now have 5 weeks vacation per year and are splitting it into 3 weeks in the summer and 2 weeks in the winter.

Farming and fishing

France is one of the world's most important agricultural countries. French farms are western Europe's leading producers of beef, veal, poultry and cheese. They also produce large quantities of milk, eggs, sugar and cereal crops, including barley and wheat.

More than 300 kinds of cheese are made in France, using milk from cows, ewes and goats. Among the best known are Camembert, Brie and Roquefort which are exported to most countries of the world.

Cattle are raised mainly in the northern and western regions of the country, particularly Brittany. Cereal crops are grown in the vast open fields of the north, especially around Paris. Fruit and vegetables come from Brittany and the warmer parts of the south. Sheep and goats are herded in the mountainous southern and eastern regions, while pigs and poultry are kept on farms all over the country.

In the past French farms were mostly very small. But during the last 30 years French agriculture has been greatly modernized to create larger and more efficient farms using fewer workers.

Above: A farmer working on a small-holding in Brittany.

Below left: A selection of the vast range of French cheeses. Nearly every village makes its own type.

Below: Some of the main breeds of French cattle. Each is named after the region where it was first raised. French breeds have been exported to many other countries. due to their fine reputation.

Charolaise

Normandy

Limousin

Above: Each wine-growing region has a different shape of bottle.
Left: Harvesting grapes by hand near Beaune, the wine capital of Burgundy. Machines are increasingly being used for this work.

Below: Unloading a fishing boat at La Turballe in Brittany. The French fishing ports on the Atlantic and Channel coasts account for over three-quarters of the French fishing catch.

Many of the changes in French farming are a result of the Common Agricultural Policy (CAP) created by the Common Market (EEC). Unfortunately this has also encouraged farmers to produce too much of some kinds of products, particularly butter, milk and wine.

France is famous for its excellent wines. Large quantities of high-quality wines are exported to all parts of the world. Among them are such well-known names as Champagne, Burgundy, Bordeaux, Beaujolais and Sauterne. Because of over-production of cheaper wines in recent years, the French government has encouraged the making of better-quality wines.

The timber industry is being promoted by the government in anticipation of a timber shortage in Europe.

The fishing industry until recently was in decline but increased investment in ships and new technology is now being made.

Natural resources and industry

France is one of the world's most important industrial nations. From its factories come such well-known French products as motor cars, aircraft, computers and spacecraft. France also has many small traditional craft industries including pottery and textiles.

The main industrial regions of France include the areas around Paris, Lille and Lyon and in Lorraine. There are also newer areas in various parts of the country where high-technology industries have developed in recent years.

France is not rich in natural resources, although it does have deposits of coal, iron ore, bauxite and other minerals. Because it produces little oil, an increasing part of the electricity needed to run the factories is now generated by nuclear power stations in various parts of the country. Research is also being done into new energy sources. A solar power plant has been in operation in the Pyrénées since 1970 and another is planned.

Below: A production line at Renault, France's largest car-making company.

Above: Large deposits of iron ore, bauxite and coal are mined in France.

Above: The symbols of France's leading car-makers.